ORDINARY
PEOPLE
CHANGE
the
WORLD

I am Marie Curie

BRAD MELTZER

illustrated by Christopher Eliopoulos

 DIAL BOOKS FOR YOUNG READERS

I am **MARIE CURIE.**

When I was four years old in Poland, this was one of my favorite treasures: my dad's glass cabinet, filled with scientific instruments. I used to stare at it, wondering about each item.

I didn't know what the words meant.
But I'd never forget them.

As a science teacher, my father needed these tools. But the Russian government soon shut down laboratory classes in our schools.

They didn't want Polish kids to learn about science. They thought education would be dangerous—that it would make us powerful.

They were right.

I really liked learning.

One day, when my older sister was struggling to read, I picked up her book and read the first sentence easily.

From the looks on everyone's faces, I thought I'd made a mistake.

Back then, men didn't think girls could be good students, and they certainly didn't think we could be scientists.
So boys were always trying to challenge me.

From the very start, there was one person who always believed in me: my dad.

When my mom got sick, he took care of us kids.

Since he was a teacher, even if we were just taking a walk, he'd give us a new scientific lesson.

Back then, we didn't have phones, TVs, or computers.

So our Saturday nights were spent with Dad sharing one of the most powerful things of all: books.

He'd read us classics like *David Copperfield* and one of my favorites, *A Tale of Two Cities*.

Growing up, life was hard.

My mom and one of my sisters passed away.

My father wasn't allowed to teach the subject he loved.

We didn't have much money.

To escape the hard times, I would read...

draw...

BOOKS WERE A PLACE WHERE I COULD ENTER ANOTHER WORLD.

and dance.

ONE NIGHT I DANCED SO LONG, I COMPLETELY WORE OUT MY SHOES.

At fifteen, I graduated from high school early.
I won the gold medal for being the first in my class.

By sixteen, I knew I wanted to make an impact on this world.
I even knew how.

There was only one problem.

Eventually, my sister Bronya and I made a plan.
We would save enough money to go to the Sorbonne in France, one of the most famous universities in the world. But we didn't have enough money for both of us.

Every day, I was so determined to become a scientist.

I'd wake up at six a.m. and read books in three different languages on physics and anatomy.

Then I'd do the math problems my dad would send for me to solve.

By the time I was eighteen, I was doing my own experiments and drawing my own conclusions.
I also learned one of the most valuable lessons of all: You should never accept everything as it is. Life, like science, can always be made better.

I felt like a new person with new power.

When I got there, I even signed the registration book differently.

CALL ME BY MY NEW NAME.

MARIE.

ENREGISTREMENT

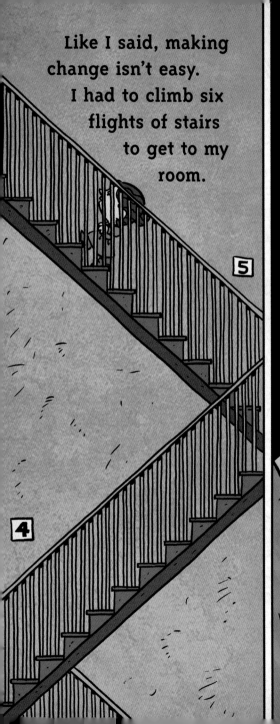

Like I said, making change isn't easy.
I had to climb six flights of stairs to get to my room.

5

4

It had a tiny stove, and there wasn't much to eat.

In the winter, it was so cold that water would freeze in the basin.

I'd have to sleep under all my clothes.

The Sorbonne's School of Science had 2,000 students. Only twenty-three were women.

And only two of us were studying science.

I was so nervous during my first exam, I could barely read it. But when the professor announced our scores...

MARIE CURIE IS FIRST IN HER CLASS!

In 1893, I got my degree in physics. A year later, I got a second degree in mathematics.

Soon after, I got married—to a scientist, of course.

THIS IS MY HUSBAND, PIERRE.

WHEN WE HAD A DAUGHTER, PEOPLE THOUGHT I WOULD SPEND LESS TIME IN THE LAB.

BUT PIERRE WORKED HARD TO MAKE SURE WE WERE EQUAL PARTNERS.

My dad helped too, by babysitting.

Back then, people thought that men were supposed to get jobs, and women were supposed to stay home.

Again, I had my own ideas.

The only thing you're *supposed* to do is chase what you love.

This was my next lab, a crowded, damp storeroom.
I started studying a chemical element called uranium.

My husband found my research so exciting, he put aside his own work to join me.

Together, we discovered two brand-new elements: polonium and radium.

Those ideas—based on my research—changed the way the world looked at atoms and radioactivity.

In 1903, I was nominated, along with my husband and another scientist named Henri Becquerel, for the Nobel Prize in Physics, one of the most prestigious awards in science.

Eventually, I became the first woman professor at the Sorbonne. Then my lab became the top place in the world for studying radium and measuring radioactivity.

In the United States, I even got invited to the White House, where President Harding presented me with one gram of radium in a locked box.

It was worth more than one hundred thousand dollars, a gift from the women in America, who'd collected money so I could continue my groundbreaking work.

SHE'S AN INSPIRATION.

SHE'S SUCH AN INSPIRATION.

In my life, I was told that
only boys could be educated,
only boys should study science,
and only boys would win awards.
I had other ideas.

Don't let anyone limit what you can achieve.
It's easy to follow the crowd and do what's been done before.
But to forge your own path, you have to be daring.
You have to risk failure.
That's how you learn.
Education is like a magic key.
It unlocks knowledge.

And with that knowledge...

Science taught me to ask questions,
experiment,
fail,
try again,
and then try some more.
You won't always find the answers you expect, and that's okay.
You will find new information, new questions, new possibilities.

ELIZABETH BLACKBURN
BIOLOGIST

SALLY RIDE
ASTRONAUT

MAE JEMISON
ASTRONAUT

GRACE HOPPER
COMPUTER SCIENTIST

DOROTHY HODGKIN
CHEMIST

I am Marie Curie.
I know the power of discovery.

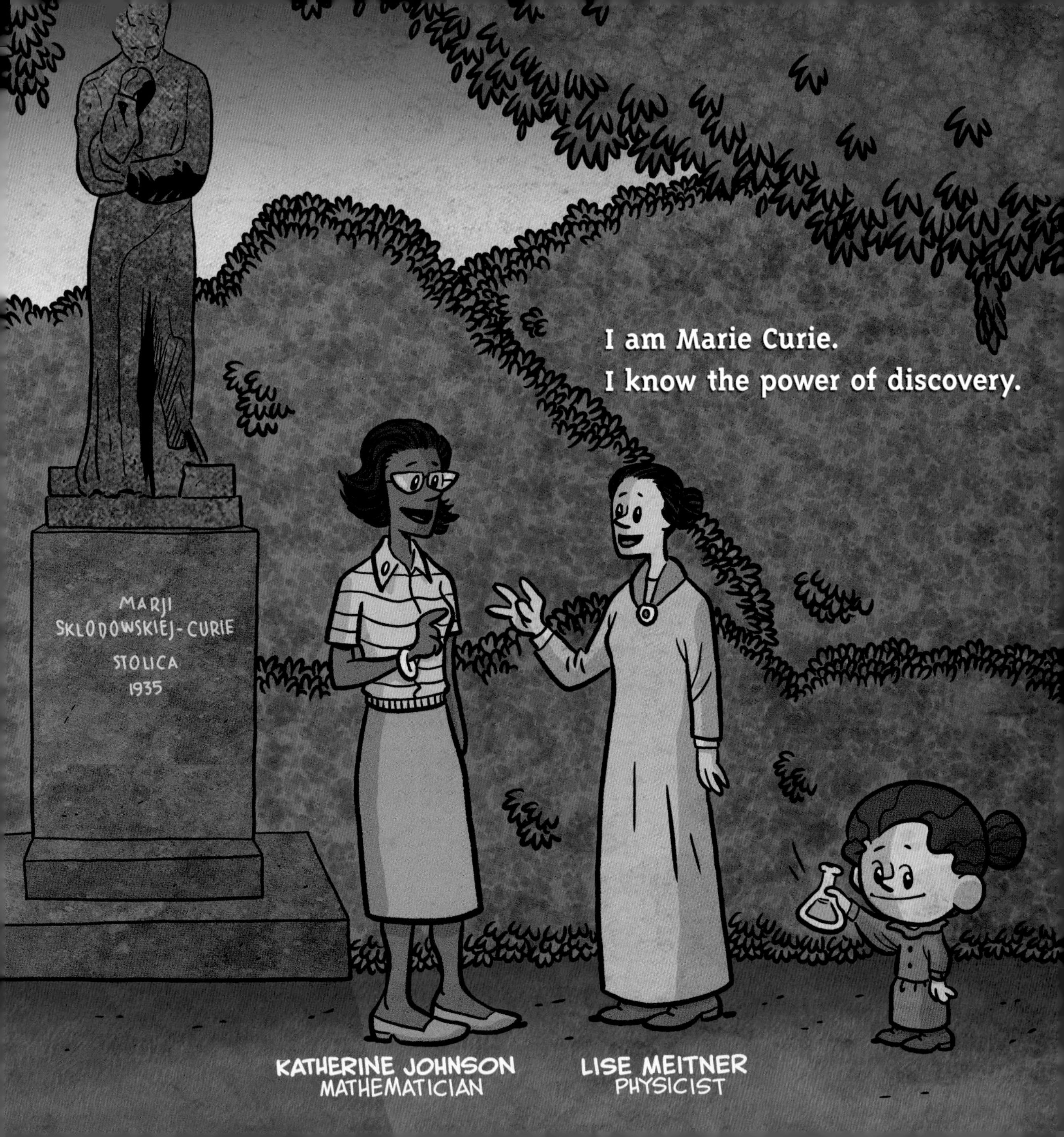

*"Nothing in life is to be feared.
It is only to be understood."*
—MARIE CURIE

Timeline

NOVEMBER 7, 1867	1891	JULY 26, 1895	JULY 18, 1898	JULY 26, 1898
Born in Warsaw, Poland, as Maria Sklodowska	Registers at the Sorbonne under the name Marie	Marries Pierre Curie	Invents the term *radioactivity* and announces discovery of polonium	Announces discovery of radium

Marie with
Pierre

Marie as a child (middle), with siblings
(left to right) Zosia, Hela, Joseph, and Bronya

Marie teaching at
the Sorbonne

Marie
in her
laboratory

DECEMBER 1903	NOVEMBER 5, 1906	1911	JULY 4, 1934	1995
Wins Nobel Prize in physics	Becomes first woman professor at the Sorbonne	Wins Nobel Prize in chemistry	Dies in France, from longtime exposure to radiation	Reburied in the French Pantheon

For Chris Weiss,
my favorite doctor.
Hope your daughters are impressed.
You owe me five bucks.
And thanks for one of the
greatest friendships of my life.
—B.M.

For Morgan and Christopher,
You can do anything,
be anything,
achieve anything.
—C.E.

SOURCES

Obsessive Genius: The Inner World of Marie Curie by Barbara Goldsmith (Norton, 2005)
Pierre Curie by Marie Curie (Dover, 2012)
Marie Curie: Mother of Modern Physics by Janice Borzendowski (Sterling, 2009)
Madame Curie—A Biography by Eve Curie
American Institute of Physics: https://history.aip.org/history/exhibits/curie/polgirl1.htm

FURTHER READING FOR KIDS

Who Was Marie Curie? by Megan Stine (Penguin Workshop, 2014)
Marie Curie by Demi (Henry Holt, 2018)
She Persisted Around the World by Chelsea Clinton (Philomel, 2018)

DIAL BOOKS FOR YOUNG READERS
An imprint of Penguin Random House LLC, New York

Text copyright © 2019 by Forty-four Steps, Inc. • Illustrations copyright © 2019 by Christopher Eliopoulos

Visit us online at penguinrandomhouse.com

LIBRARY OF CONGRESS CATALOGING-IN-PUBLICATION DATA
Names: Meltzer, Brad, author. | Eliopoulos, Chris, illustrator. | Title: I am Marie Curie / by Brad Meltzer ; illustrated by Christopher Eliopoulos.
Other titles: Ordinary people change the world.
Description: New York : Dial Books for Young Readers, [2019] | Series: Ordinary people change the world | "Dial Books for Young Readers: an imprint of Penguin Random House LLC."
Audience: Ages 5–8. | Audience: K to grade 3. | Identifiers: LCCN 2019008249 | ISBN 9780525555858 (hardcover) | Subjects: LCSH: Curie, Marie, 1867–1934—Juvenile literature.
Radioactivity—History—Juvenile literature. | Women chemists—France—Biography—Juvenile literature. | Women physicists—France—Biography—Juvenile literature.
Chemists—France—Biography—Juvenile literature. | Physicists—France—Biography—Juvenile literature. | Women Nobel Prize winners—Biography—Juvenile literature.
Nobel Prize winners—Biography—Juvenile literature. | Classification: LCC QD22.C8 M45 2019 | DDC 540.92—dc23 LC | record available at https://lccn.loc.gov/2019008249

Manufactured in China on acid-free paper • 10 9 8 7 6 5 4 3 2 1

Designed by Jason Henry • Text set in Triplex • The artwork for this book was created digitally.